BYRON BECK

DIKEMBE MUTOMBO

DAVID THOMPSON

RAEF LaFRENTZ

DAN ISSEL

ALEX ENGLISH

ANTONIO McDYESS

KIKI VANDEWEGHE

FAT LEVER

LaPHONSO ELLIS

SPENCER HAYWOOD

NICK VAN EXEL

CREATIVE C EDUCATION

AARON FRISCH

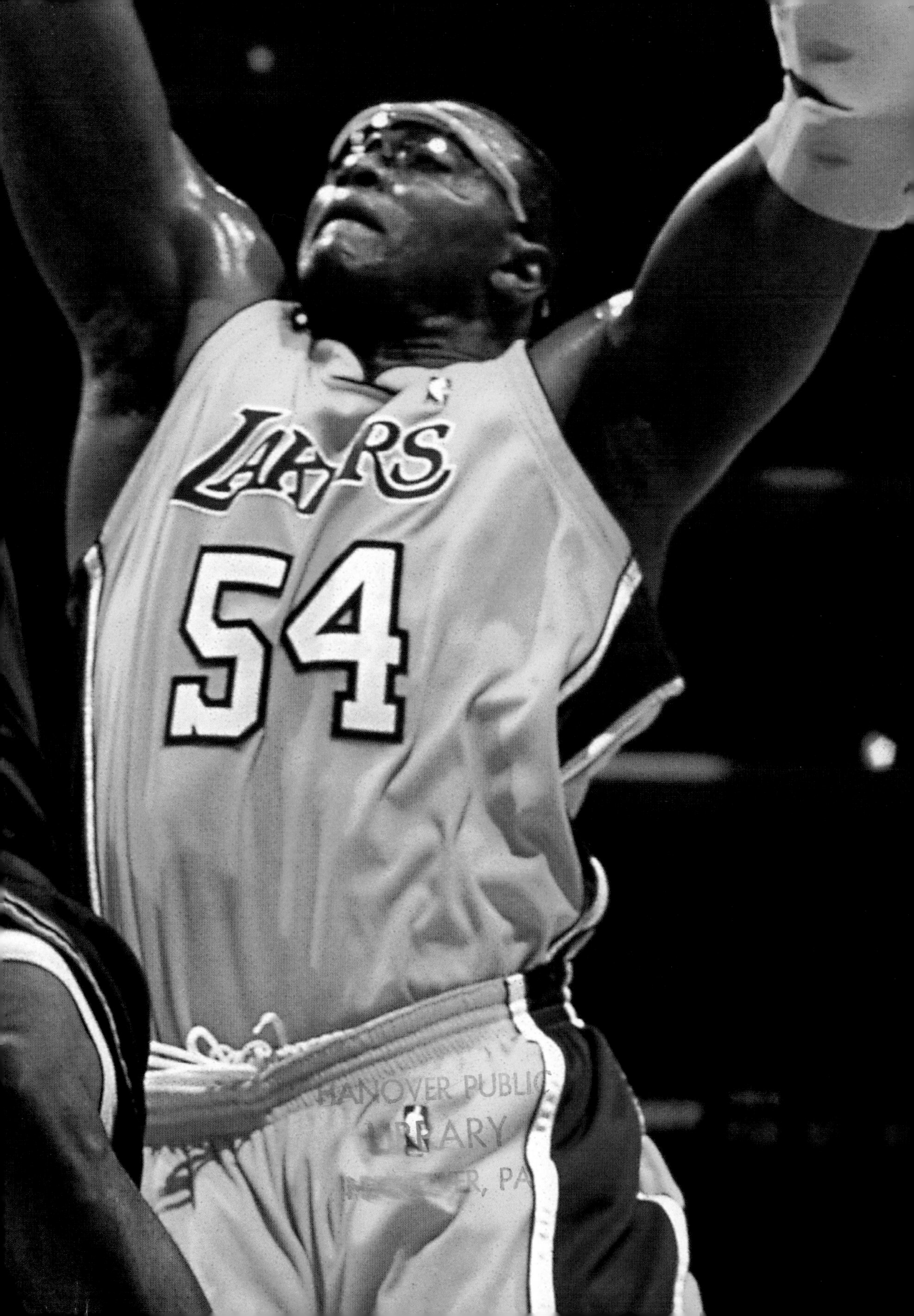
54

Published by Creative Education, 123 South Broad Street, Mankato, MN 56001

Creative Education is an imprint of The Creative Company.

Design and Art Direction by Rita Marshall

Photos by Allsport, NBA Photos

Library of Congress Cataloging-in-Publication Data

Frisch, Aaron. The history of the Denver Nuggets / by Aaron Frisch.

p. cm. – (Pro basketball today)   ISBN 1-58341-096-1   1. Denver Nuggets (Basketball team)—History—

Juvenile literature. [1. Denver Nuggets (Basketball team)—History. 2. Basketball—History.] I. Title. II. Series.

GV885.52.D45 F75 2001   796.323'64'0978883—dc21   00-047342

First Edition 9 8 7 6 5 4 3 2 1

DENVER, COLORADO, RANKS AS ONE OF AMERICA'S MOST BEAUTIFUL CITIES. SETTLED HIGH IN THE

foothills of the Rocky Mountains, it is known as the "Mile High City."

Denver owes its existence in large part to gold and silver. Founded by

prospectors, the city grew rapidly during the 1870s when large deposits

of these precious metals were found nearby.

Today, valuable metals continue to play a prominent role in

Denver. Half of all U.S. coins are minted here. Denver also boasts a pro-

fessional basketball team named for the gold nuggets that put the city

on the map. The Nuggets franchise was born in 1967 as a member of

WILLIE MURRELL

the upstart American Basketball Association (ABA), and it quickly became the pride of Denver.

{THE ROCKETS ARE LAUNCHED} The Nuggets started out in 1967 as the Denver Rockets, one of the original teams in the ABA. Their first coach was Bob Bass, formerly a successful small-college coach. "[Denver general manager Dennis] Murphy offered me $20,000 to coach

6 in Denver, which was pretty good money since most of the players would be making about $8,000," explained Bass. "So I took the job."

Like its coach, most of Denver's players that first season were unknowns. About the only one fans had heard of was forward Wayne Hightower, who had played several seasons in the National Basketball Association (NBA). Playing home games in the small Denver Auditorium, the Rockets had a fine first season, finishing 45–33.

ANTONIO McDYESS

Spencer Haywood became an ABA super-star in his first pro season.

SPENCER HAYWOOD

A year later, Denver made a bold move, offering a contract to a phenomenal 19-year-old forward named Spencer Haywood. The offer created controversy because Haywood was just a sophomore at the University of Detroit, and there was an unwritten rule that pro teams would not approach college players until they graduated. The young star's decision to sign with Denver was an historic turning point in basketball, as other outstanding undergraduates soon began turning pro early as well.

Forward Byron Beck was a steady low-post presence throughout Denver's ABA years.

9

Haywood had a huge impact on the ABA. In only his first season, he led the league in scoring and rebounding and was named Most Valuable Player. Led by the star forward, the Rockets won their division with a 51–33 record and reached the second round of the playoffs. The team also drew big crowds, helping Denver make money at a time when

BYRON BECK

Like Spencer Haywood, Reggie Williams was a quick and versatile forward.

REGGIE WILLIAMS

most ABA teams were struggling financially.

Sadly, the Rockets' new-found glory didn't last. After playing just

Young guard
Ralph Simpson
emerged as an
ABA All-Star
in **1971–72**,
netting 27
points per
game.
one season in Denver, Haywood decided to join the

NBA's Seattle SuperSonics. Without him, the Rockets fell

to last place in their division in 1970–71.

{THE SKYWALKER LEAPS TO DENVER} In 1974,

Denver brought in two new leaders: general manager

Carl Scheer and coach Larry Brown. Scheer quickly made two important

changes. First, he moved the team to a bigger home—the 17,000-seat

McNichols Sports Arena. Then, having decided that the team needed a

new identity, he held a contest to find a new team name. The winning

suggestion was Nuggets.

"Bringing in Carl Scheer and Larry Brown probably saved the

Denver franchise . . . ," said Denver center Dave Robisch. "When they

BOBBY JONES

came to town, the Broncos [football team] owned the city, and there was

serious apathy about the basketball club. We lost our first game [in

1974–75], and nobody seemed to notice. But when we won our next

nine in a row, people starting packing the arena, and we became the

hottest ticket in town."

The Nuggets earned Denver's attention for good reason. The team that had gone 37–47 the previous season suddenly seemed unstoppable, jumping to an ABA-record 65–19 mark. Coach Brown had assembled a talented lineup that was led by guard Mack Calvin, a great ball handler. Ralph Simpson teamed up with Calvin in the backcourt, while big men Byron Beck, Dave Robisch, and rookie Bobby Jones anchored the frontcourt.

> Mack Calvin led Denver's record-setting **1974–75** team with nearly eight assists per game.

The Nuggets lost to the Indiana Pacers in the 1975 playoffs, but they moved a step closer to an ABA championship by drafting star swingman David Thompson in the off-season. Thompson, a two-time College Player of the Year at North Carolina, was nicknamed "the Skywalker" because of his amazing jumping ability. The Nuggets scored a major victory when Thompson signed with them instead of the Atlanta Hawks, who had made him the first pick in the NBA's annual draft.

"Denver had a great franchise, and I knew Carl Scheer and Larry

14

DAVID THOMPSON

Brown from North Carolina," Thompson said. "So the Nuggets were a natural [fit] for me. Atlanta wasn't in good shape back then. Really, it was an easy choice. It didn't matter that Denver was in the ABA,

because the Nuggets were very 'big league.'"

With Thompson on board, the excitement rose even higher in Denver. But Thompson wasn't the only new face in town. The Nuggets had also traded for forward Dan Issel. Although Issel didn't have

Thompson's raw talent, he was one of the hardest-working players in

the league. Known as "the Horse," he was a tough

rebounder and a steady scorer.

{GETTING OFFENSIVE IN THE NBA} With

Thompson and Issel leading the charge, Denver posted

the ABA's best record again in 1975–76 with a 60–24

mark. The Nuggets drove as far as the league finals before falling to

"Dr. J" (Julius Erving) and the New York Nets. It was to be the ABA's

final championship.

By 1976, the ABA was in trouble. Attendance was generally low,

and the league had been unable to land a national television contract.

Still, the league had some of the game's best players, so the NBA decid-

ed to add some of the ABA's top teams and stars. Denver was one of the

Forward Dan Issel grabbed more rebounds than any other Nuggets player in history.

DAN ISSEL

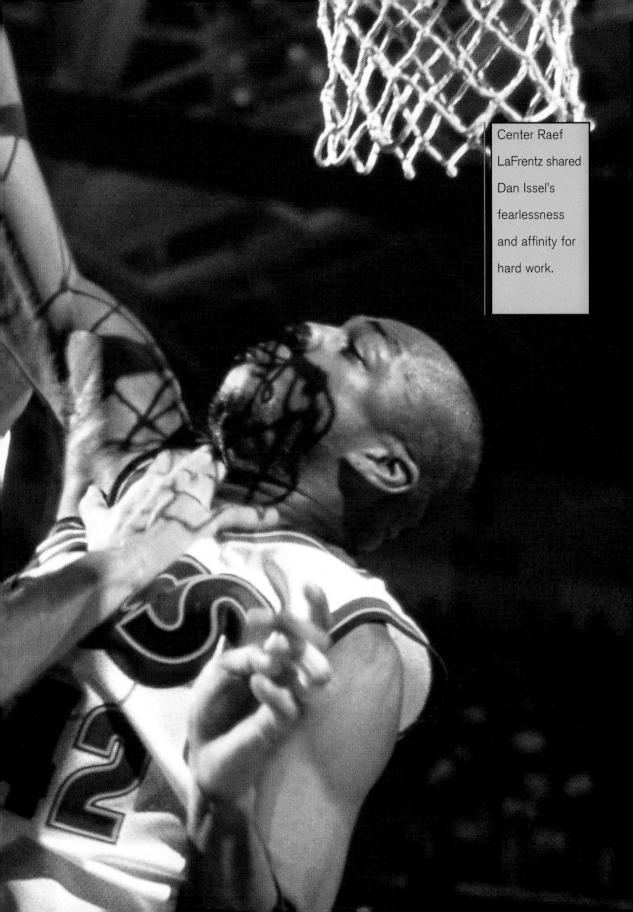

Center Raef LaFrentz shared Dan Issel's fearlessness and affinity for hard work.

teams invited to join the NBA, along with the New York Nets, San

Antonio Spurs, and Indiana Pacers.

Alex
English
scored more
points in the
'80s than
any other
player in the
league.

The Nuggets proved that they belonged among the

NBA's best by going 50–32 and winning the Midwest

Division in 1976–77. But Larry Brown stepped down as

coach in 1978, and Denver faded in the standings. In

1979–80, the Nuggets went a mere 30–52. The season's

20 only highlight was the addition of Alex English, a high-scoring guard

previously with Indiana.

After the Nuggets got off to a slow start the next year, former

assistant coach Doug Moe took the head coaching reins. Moe was

known for his sarcastic sense of humor and wide-open style of offense.

"Moe had no set plays, ran short practices that were primarily condition-

ing drills, and told his players to shoot whenever they wanted," noted

ALEX ENGLISH

NBA writer Zander Hollander.

With the offense-minded Moe in control, Denver boasted some of

the league's top scorers. Thompson, English, Issel, and forward Kiki

Vandeweghe all burned up the nets throughout the early 1980s.

Unfortunately, the Nuggets' defense was not nearly as strong. In 1983–84,

Denver once scored 184 points in a game—and still lost (186–184 to

Detroit). Fans packed McNichols Arena to watch the Nuggets' high-octane offense, but the team was ousted early from the playoffs every year.

In **1984–85**, guard Mike Evans led Denver's long-range attack with 57 three-pointers.

{A NEW ERA WITH FAT} In 1984, Denver began to rebuild its lineup. In a major trade, the Nuggets sent the high-scoring Vandeweghe to Portland for three players— forward Calvin Natt, center Wayne Cooper, and guard Lafayette "Fat" Lever. Nuggets fans were at first furious over losing Vandeweghe, but the move paid off. The reshaped Nuggets lineup went 52–30 and drove all the way to the conference finals in 1985 before losing to the Los Angeles Lakers.

The players acquired in the Vandeweghe trade all made major contributions that season. Natt averaged 23 points per game, and Cooper emerged as a dominant shot blocker. Lever, meanwhile, gave the Nuggets valuable leadership and aggressive defense. "Fat Lever has all of these

MIKE EVANS

Center
Wayne Cooper
averaged 166
blocked shots
per season
from **1984–85**
to **1988–89**.

WAYNE COOPER

'plus' factors . . . ," said Dallas coach Richie Adubato. "[He's a] fierce competitor, best rebounding guard in the league, great defensive player, great assist man, and good scorer."

In 1986–87, injuries to Natt and Cooper knocked Denver down in the standings. But the Nuggets stormed back the next year with a 54–28 record. Part of their success was due to newcomer Michael Adams. The 5-foot-9 guard, obtained in a trade with Washington, had great speed and was a terrific defender. He also had a deadly outside shooting touch and launched hundreds of three-point bombs.

Despite standing just 6-foot-3, Fat Lever led Denver with nearly nine boards per game in **1986–87**.

The Nuggets now had a talented backcourt, but Issel had retired, and the team was undersized and overmatched at the forward and center positions. Unable to match the physical strength of many teams, Denver found little success in the playoffs.

FAT LEVER

{MUTOMBO MAKES HIS MARK} In 1990, a new group of

owners took over the Nuggets and hired former NBA coach Bernie

Bickerstaff as general manager. Bickerstaff quickly overhauled the team,

letting English leave as a free agent and sending Lever to Dallas in

exchange for draft picks. Moe then stepped down as coach and was

replaced by Paul Westhead.

These changes resulted in an NBA-worst 20–62 record in 1990–91.

The team's shakeup continued as Adams and veteran center Blair

Rasmussen were then traded away for high picks in the

1991 NBA Draft. The Nuggets used one of those picks

to select towering center Dikembe Mutombo.

Over the next few seasons, Mutombo developed

into one of the best centers in the league. Though his

offensive skills were unspectacular, Mutombo excelled at other abilities

his college coach—John Thompson of Georgetown—had encouraged him

to develop. "Son," Thompson told him, "you will make millions and mil-

lions of dollars more than people who score if you can play defense,

which means two things—rebounding and blocking shots."

Along with point guard Mahmoud Abdul-Rauf—another young

player drafted in the early '90s—Mutombo led Denver to one of its

Quick guard Mahmoud Abdul-Rauf was Denver's top scoring threat in the mid-**1990s**.

MAHMOUD ABDUL-RAUF

greatest moments ever in the 1994 playoffs. The Nuggets had earned

the last playoff spot in the Western Conference and faced the Seattle

SuperSonics, owners of the NBA's best record. Seattle

won the first two games, but Mutombo dominated the

paint in the next three as Denver pulled off one of the

biggest upsets in NBA history.

Mutombo and Abdul-Rauf led the team again the next

season with the help of forward LaPhonso Ellis. But when Ellis was side-

lined with nagging injuries, Denver brought in another talented young

forward named Antonio McDyess. With long arms, a muscular build,

and great leaping ability, the 6-foot-9 McDyess was capable of dominat-

ing players of all sizes at both ends of the floor.

Still, the Nuggets posted a mediocre record in 1995–96. Then, one

by one, Denver's stars left town. Mutombo went to Atlanta as a free

*LaPhonso Ellis teamed up with Dikembe Mutombo to block 16 shots in one **1994** playoff game.*

28

LaPHONSO ELLIS

agent, and Abdul-Rauf was soon traded to Sacramento. Unwilling to pay

McDyess the large contract he was seeking, the Nuggets traded him to

Phoenix a year later. Without their three best players,

the Nuggets fell apart. In 1997–98, under new coach Bill

Hanzlik, they posted an embarrassing 11–71 record.

{A MILE HIGH WITH McDYESS} Fortunately,

an unexpected hero soon arrived to turn things around.

In **1998–99**, guard Chauncey Billups drained 64 consecutive free throws at McNichols Arena.

Unhappy with his role in Phoenix, McDyess returned to Denver as a

free agent in 1998. "I just felt more comfortable with the Nuggets

organization and the city of Denver," McDyess explained. "I guess I

wanted the pressure of being a leader."

McDyess didn't have to bear that pressure alone, however. The

Nuggets had also added two other fine young players. The first was

point guard Nick Van Exel, a slick playmaker previously with the Los

CHAUNCEY BILLUPS

Nick Van
Exel's slashing
style and
great court
vision made
him a superb
playmaker.

NICK VAN EXEL

With Raef LaFrentz working the boards, the Nuggets rose in the standings in **1999–00**.

RAEF LaFRENTZ

Angeles Lakers. The second was Raef LaFrentz, a hardworking center

picked up in the 1998 NBA Draft. These players, along with shooting

Denver added
to its outside
firepower by
trading for
sharpshooter
Voshon
Lenard in
2000–01. guard Bryant Stith, formed a promising lineup.

In 1999–00, the Nuggets found a new home in

Denver's state-of-the-art Pepsi Center. Former Nuggets

forward and local hero Dan Issel also took over as coach,

guiding his young team to an improved 35–47 record.

32 Late in the season, the Nuggets continued to build for the future by

adding versatile young guard Tariq Abdul-Wahad.

Over the years, the Nuggets have boasted some of basketball's

greatest scorers and most spectacular players. Yet as thrilling as Denver

basketball has been, the team continues to seek its first NBA title.

Today's Nuggets hope to soon capture that title and add the precious

metal of a league championship trophy to the Mile High City.

VOSHON LENARD